Events

News for ever...

The first CAMRA (Campaign for Real Ale)
National Beer Exhibition is held in London
from 9-13 September.

By Hugh Morrison

MONTPELIER PUBLISHING

Front cover (clockwise from left): Lynda Carter first appears on TV as Wonder Woman on 7 November. The TV series *Space 1999* is first broadcast on 1 September. The film *Jaws* is released on 20 June. Johnny Rotten of the Sex Pistols, who give their first concert on 5 November. The Vauxhall Cavalier, launched on 14 October.

Rear cover (clockwise from left): General Franco of Spain dies on 20 November. Haile Selassie, Emperor of Ethiopia, dies on 27 August. Pelé makes his US football debut on 16 June. The AMC Pacer is launched on 28 February. Margaret Thatcher becomes leader of the Conservative Party on 11 February. Rod Stewart hits number one in the charts with *Sailing* on 6 September.

Image credits: Christopher Ziemnowicz, Cameron Roxberry, Charles O1, Erlin Mandelmann, Elektra Publicity, Seb Morgan, American Museum of Natural History, London Fire Brigade, Kitmaster Bloke, Erwin Lux, Georges Biard, GillPhoto, Allan Warren, Ted Quackenbush, Rob Bogaerts.

Published in Great Britain by Montpelier Publishing.
This edition © 2024. All rights reserved.
www.hughmorrisonbooks.com
ISBN: 9798340996251

January 1975

Wednesday 1: In the Queen's New Year Honours, Charlie Chaplin, PG Wodehouse, Roger Bannister and Gareth Sobers receive knighthoods.

Thursday 2: The World Tourism Organisation is established by the United Nations.

Friday 3: The largest return of land by the US government to American Indians takes place when 250 square miles of territory is ceded to the Havasupai tribe in Arizona.

Charlie Chaplin is knighted on 1 January.

Saturday 4: The temporary 55 mph speed limit in the USA becomes permanent.

The cartoonist Bob Montana, creator of Archie Comics, dies aged 54.

Sunday 5: 12 people are killed when the freighter *Lake Illawarra* hits the Tasman Bridge in Tasmania, Australia.

Monday 6: The game show *Wheel of Fortune* is first broadcast on US TV.

Tuesday 7: In the Vietnam War, the first South Vietnamese

January 1975

province is captured by the Viet Cong.

Wednesday 8: Following the lack of a US response to the previous day's attack on South Vietnam (US forces withdrew in 1973) the Viet Cong begins a full scale invasion of the south.

Thursday 9: Australia beats England by 171 runs to regain the Ashes in cricket's fourth Test in Sydney.

Friday 10: Bernadette Olowo becomes the first female Papal Envoy (Vatican ambassador).

The *Queen Elizabeth II* liner begins its first round-the-world cruise.

Face of evil: serial killer Ted Bundy claims his 15th victim on 12 January.

Saturday 11: Soviet cosmonauts Gubarev and Grechko begin a record 28 day mission on the the space station Salyut 4.

Sunday 12: Caryn Campbell of Snowmass, Colorado, becomes the fifteenth victim of serial killer Ted Bundy.

Monday 13: Arab terrorists attempt to blow up an El Al airliner at Orly Airport, Paris, using a surface to air missile. The attempt fails but destroys an empty Yugoslavian aircraft nearby.

The *QE2* begins its first round the world cruise on 10 January

Tuesday 14: The House Un-American Activities Committee, famous for its anti-communist 'witch-hunts' under Senator McCarthy, is disbanded after 37 years.

January 1975

Above: Isabel Sanford, Sherman Hemsley and Mike Evans star in *The Jeffersons*, first broadcast on 18 January.

Lesley Whittle, 17, is kidnapped by Donald Neilson, alias the Black Panther in Highley, Shropshire. In March Lesley is found dead in a drainage shaft in Bathpool Park, Staffs; Neilson is arrested in December and sentenced to life imprisonment.

Wednesday 15: The Algor Agreement is signed, granting the colony of Angola independence from Portugal by 11 November 1975.

Thursday 16: The 199th and final episode of the US crime series *Ironside*, starring Raymond Burr, is broadcast.

Friday 17: Abortion on demand is legalised in France.

Saturday 18: The long-running US sitcom *The Jeffersons* is first broadcast.

27 people are killed in a train derailment near Cairo, Egypt.

Sunday 19: An Arab terror attack and hostage crisis takes place at Orly Airport, Paris; 78 people are injured and the three terrorists are allowed to escape to Iraq.

Monday 20: After only a year, construction on the Channel Tunnel between England and France is cancelled due to mounting costs. The tunnel is completed privately in 1994.

Raymond Burr makes his final appearance as Chief Ironside on 16 January.

January 1975

On 30 January Erno Rubik files a patent for a puzzle which is later marketed as Rubik's Cube.

Tuesday 21: Lily Crossley, 73, becomes the first victim of serial killer Dr Harold Shipman in Todmorden, West Yorkshire. Two more of his patients are killed on the same day. 25 years later he is convicted of 215 murders, and implicated in 200 more.

Wednesday 22: Aston Villa defeats Norwich City to win the Football League Cup at Wembley Stadium, London.

Thursday 23: Dr Andreas Gruentzig performs the first angioplasty (artery and vein obstruction removal) on a dog. In 1976 he performs the technique successfully on a human patient.

Friday 24: Comedian Larry Fine of the Three Stooges dies aged 72.

The jazz pianist Keith Jarrett performs the Koln Concert in Cologne, Germany. The recording becomes the best selling piano recording of all time.

Saturday 25: Jack Nicholson is awarded a Golden Globe for *Chinatown*, which is also nominated as Best Motion Picture in the awards.

Sunday 26: RAF Cadet Edward Wilson, 16, is killed in an IRA bomb attack on an Air Training Corps barracks in Belfast.

Keith Jarrett makes the world's best selling piano recording on 24 January.

Monday 27: The House of Commons rejects proposals to make

January 1975

Jack Nicholson is awarded a Golden Globe on 25 January.

Welsh words on road signs in Wales in a different colour to those in English.

Tuesday 28: Japan and the USSR sign a joint agreement on oil drilling in Sakhalin Island.

Wednesday 29: The far-left terror group The Weather Underground carries out a bomb attack on the US State Department in Washington, DC.

Thursday 30: Professor Erno Rubik of Budapest, Hungary, applies for the patent on his 'spatial logic game', later to become famous as Rubik's Cube.

Friday 31: The last victim of the serial killer known as the Skid Row Slasher is claimed in Hollywood, California. The perpetrator, Vaughn Greenwood, is convicted two years later.

February 1975

Saturday 1: US President Gerald Ford announces the country has the largest fiscal deficit in its peacetime history.

Sunday 2: Dorothy Hamill, 18, wins the US ladies' figure skating championships.

Monday 3: Eli Black, the chief executive of the US corporation United Brands, commits suicide in New York City. It is later revealed he paid a $1.25m bribe to a Honduran government minister to prevent a tax on his company's products.

Tuesday 4: The former British Prime Minister Edward Heath steps down as leader of the Conservative Party.

The rock-and-roll pioneer Louis Jordan dies aged 66.

The actress and singer Natalie Imbruglia is born in Sydney, Australia.

Wednesday 5: 100 people die during a state of emergency in Peru caused by a two-day police strike.

Right: Louis Jordan (shown here in 1946) dies on 4 February.

February 1975

Natalie Imbruglia (shown here in 2008) is born on 4 February.

Thursday 6: Sir Keith Park, Air Chief Marshal of the Royal Air Force during the Battle of Britain, dies aged 82.

The luxury British car manufacturer Jensen announces it is cutting two-thirds of its workforce.

Friday 7: The *Los Angeles Times* reveals the existence of Project Azorian, a US government secret attempt to raise the Soviet submarine *K-129* which sank in the Pacific in 1968.

Saturday 8: A group of nine Cornishmen issue a unilateral declaration of independence from Great Britain. Bus conductor Brian Hamblet leads the group, styling himself 'Lord Protector'. Cornwall was originally a separate country, but came under English rule in the ninth century AD.

Sunday 9: The cosmonauts Georgi Grechko and Alexsei Gubarev return to Earth after a record one month in space on board the Salyut 4 space station.

Monday 10: A ceasefire between the Provisional Irish Republican Army and British forces is declared in Northern Ireland; it lasts until January 1976.

Tuesday 11: Margaret Thatcher is elected as head of Britain's Conservative Party.

Left: A Jensen Interceptor. The troubled car manufacturer announces major redundancies on 6 February.

February 1975

Above: Margaret Thatcher becomes leader of the Conservative Party on 11 February. Below: Olivia Newton-John receives an award on 18 February.

Wednesday 12: Voters in South Korea decide in favour of the provisional Yushin Constitution launched in 1972.

Thursday 13: A major fire breaks out on the North Tower of the World Trade Center in New York City.

The Turkish Federated State of Cyprus under Rauf Denktas is declared; it is not recognised by the international community.

Friday 14: The author P.G. Wodehouse, creator of Jeeves and Wooster, dies aged 93.

The biologist Julian Huxley, brother of the author Aldous Huxley, dies aged 87.

Saturday 15: The first acquisition of new US territory in 50 years takes place when the Northern Maraiana Islands in the Pacific come under American control.

Sunday 16: The South African government announces it is withdrawing support for Rhodesia's white minority government; this leads in part to the fall of white Rhodesia in 1979.

Monday 17: The Australian heavy metal band AC/DC releases its first album, *High Voltage.*

The film director George E. Marshall dies aged 83.

Tuesday 18: The footballer Gary Neville is born in Bury, Greater Manchester.

February 1975

Olivia Newton-John and John Denver receive accolades in the 2nd American Music Awards.

Wednesday 19: The US Freedom of Information Act is reformed.

Thursday 20: A feud breaks out between rival terror groups The Irish Republican Army (IRA) and the Irish National Liberation Army (INLA).

Gerald Ford on the golf course. On 26 February he becomes the first US President to play in a PGA tournament.

Friday 21: The former US Attorney General John N. Mitchell is sentenced to two and a half years in prison over his involvement in the Watergate Scandal.

Saturday 22: 27 people are killed in a train crash at Tretten in Norway.

The actress Drew Barrymore (*ET: the Extra Terrestrial*) is born in Culver City, California.

Sunday 23: Daylight Saving Time begins in the USA two months early due to the energy crisis.

Monday 24: Representatives of 58 nations attend the coronation of King Birenda of Nepal in Khatmandu.

The AMC Pacer is launched on 28 February.

February 1975

King Birenda of Nepal is crowned on 24 February.

Tuesday 25: West Germany reverses its 1974 legalisation of abortion on demand.

Wednesday 26: Gerald Ford becomes the first US President to take part in a PGA golf tournament at the Inverrary Classic in Florida.

Thursday 27: Peter Lorenz, leader of West Germany's Christian Democratic Union party, is kidnapped by anarchists in West Berlin. He is released unharmed on 4 March.

The largest and longest-burning fire in New York City history breaks out at the main telephone exchange in Manhattan.

Friday 28: 43 people are killed in London Underground's worst disaster, when a train crashes into a wall at Moorgate station.

An injured passenger is held by firemen as doctors perform emergency surgery in the wreckage of a tube carriage following the Moorgate crash of 28 February.

March 1975

Saturday 1: Colour TV broadcasting begins in Australia.

Aston Villa beats Norwich City 1-0 to win the Football League final at Wembley Stadium, London.

Sunday 2: The Shah of Iran declares his kingdom to be a one-party state.

Monday 3: The first women 'Mounties' begin service in the Royal Canadian Mounted Police.

Tuesday 4: The comedian Charlie Chaplin is knighted by HM Queen Elizabeth II at Buckingham Palace.

The villain Davros first appears on TV on 8 February.

Wednesday 5: Eight hostages and three Israeli soldiers are killed when Arab terrorists attack the Savoy Hotel in Tel Aviv.

Thursday 6: Iran and Iraq sign a peace treaty.

Friday 7: The 114th and final episode of the sitcom *The Odd Couple* is broadcast on US TV.

Saturday 8: The character of Davros, evil leader of the Daleks, first appears in the BBC sci-fi series *Dr Who*.

March 1975

The *Golden Hinde II* in London. On 9 March the replica ship arrives in San Francisco.

Sunday 9: The *Golden Hinde II*, the replica of Sir Francis Drake's ship, arrives in San Francisco after following the route of his voyage from Plymouth, England, in 1579.

Monday 10: Half of South Vietnam's territory is seized in a major offensive by North Vietnamese troops, marking the beginning of the end for the free south.

Tuesday 11: A failed coup attempt takes place in Portugal.

Wednesday 12: The last conscripted men are called up for service in the US forces. From 1 April only volunteers are recruited.

Thursday 13: The romantic comedy *Same Time, Next Year* by Bernard Slade opens on Broadway. It runs for 1453 performances.

Friday 14: South Vietnam's leader, President Thieu, decides to abandon the territory seized by North Vietnamese forces on 10 March, beginning a major evacuation.

Saturday 15: The German space probe Helios 1 makes the closest approach of any man made object to the sun up to this date, coming within 28.7 million miles (46.2 million km).

The long running sitcom *The Odd Couple* starring Tony Randall (left) and Jack Klugman ends on 7 March.

March 1975

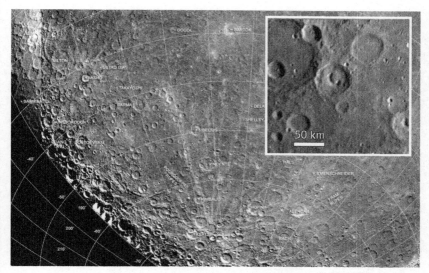

Above: Mariner 10 sends back photos from its closest approach to Mercury on 16 March, including close-ups of features such as the Beckett Crater (inset).

The shipping magnate Aristotle Onassis, husband of former First Lady Jackie Kennedy, dies aged 69.

Sunday 16: The Mariner 10 satellite makes the closest ever approach to Mercury up to this date, returning photographs of the planet's surface.

Monday 17: The first Television Electronic Disc (TeD) videorecorders are launched in West Germany. A rival to VHS and Betamax, it is unpopular due to its limited recording times.

Tuesday 18: The black majority leader in Rhodesia, Herbert Chitepo, is assassinated in a car bomb attack.

Aristotle Onassis dies on 15 March.

Wednesday 19: The second largest city in South Vietnam, Hue, is evacuated as North Vietnamese troops move rapidly southwards.

March 1975

Left: Netherlands group Teach-In wins the Eurovision Song Contest on 22 March.

Thursday 20: The Invalid Care Allowance is introduced in England and Wales as part of the Social Security Act 1975.

Friday 21: The far-left junta who seized control of Ethiopia in 1974 announce that is to abolish the Ethiopian Empire, dating from 950BC.

Saturday 22: The Eurovision Song Contest is won by the Netherlands, with *Ding-A-Dong* sung by Teach-In.

Sunday 23: Jean Guery, the French ambassador to Somalia, is kidnapped. French authorities pay the demanded ransom of $100,000 in gold.

Monday 24: A relatively unknown boxer, Chuck Wepner, comes close to beating the world heavyweight champion Muhammed Ali in Cleveland, Ohio. Wepner, beaten in the fifteenth round, is the inspiration for the Sylvester Stallone film *Rocky*.

Alexander Mitchell, 50, of King's Lynn, Norfolk, literally dies laughing while watching an episode of the BBC comedy series *The Goodies*.

Tuesday 25: King Faisal of Saudi Arabia is assassinated by his nephew, Prince Faisal bin Musaid.

March 1975

Wednesday 26: The Biological Weapons Convention comes into force.

British Leyland launches its new Morris 18-22 saloon to replace the Austin 1800.

Thursday 27: Construction begins on the Alaska Pipeline.

The rapper 'Fergie' (Stacy Ferguson) is born in Hacienda Heights, California.

Labelle hits number one on 29 March.

Friday 28 (Good Friday): The political scientist Ernst Fraenkel dies aged 76.

Saturday 29: *Lady Marmalade* by Labelle hits number one in the US singles charts.

Sunday 30 (Easter Sunday): The 'Easter Sunday Massacre' takes place when James Ruppert kills eleven members of his own family in Hamilton, Ohio. He is later declared insane.

Monday 31: The 635th and final episode of the western series *Gunsmoke* is broadcast on US TV.

Lon Nol, President of Cambodia, flees the country as Khmer Rouge communists come close to seizing power.

The Morris 18-22 (later named the Austin Princess) is launched on 26 March.

April 1975

Tuesday 1: Saukam Khoy becomes Acting President of Cambodia following the flight of Lon Nol the previous day.

Wednesday 2: Canada's CN Tower is completed, making it the world's tallest free standing structure at 1,185 feet (553m) high.

Thursday 3: US President Ford orders the evacuation of all US citizens from Pnomh Penh as the communist insurgency nears the Cambodian capital.

The film *Monty Python and the Holy Grail* is released in the UK.

Friday 4: 138 people are killed and 175 survive when a Vietnamese humanitarian airlift plane, part of Operation Babylift, crashes near Tan Son Nhut.

Bill Gates and Paul Allen incorporate the Microsoft computer company in Albuquerque, New Mexico.

Saturday 5: The Soviet rocket Soyuz 18a crash

The CN Tower is completed on 2 April.

April 1975

Left: Graham Chapman stars in *Monty Python and the Holy Grail*, released on 3 April.

lands shortly after take-off. The two cosmonauts on board are able to escape safely.

Chang Kai-Shek, President of the Republic of China (Taiwan) dies aged 87.

Sunday 6: Yen Chia-Kan becomes President of Taiwan.

Monday 7: Cambodia's Prime Minister, Long Boret, is offered the chance to flee the country by Khmer Rouge communist rebels. He refuses, and is executed nine days later.

Tuesday 8: The jazz dancer Josephine Baker gives her last public performance.

Art Carney wins Best Actor for *Harry and Tonto* at the Academy Awards. *The Godfather Part II* becomes the first sequel to win Best Picture.

Bill Gates' Microsoft company is incorporated on 4 April.

April 1975

Left: Maronite (Christian) troops engage in the Lebanon Civil War, which breaks out on 13 April.

Wednesday 9: The Indian Army invades Sikkim at the behest of the Prime Minister. 400 royal guards are disarmed and the King is placed under house arrest.

Joey, the world's oldest canary, dies aged 34 in Hull, Yorkshire.

Thursday 10: The legislature of Sikkim votes to abolish the monarchy.

Friday 11: North Vietnam seizes the disputed Spratly Islands in the South China sea, which action eventually leads to war with China in 1979.

Saturday 12: The jazz dancer Josephine Baker dies aged 68.

Sunday 13: Civil war between Muslims and Christians begins in Lebanon.

Monday 14: The first 'no frills' airline goes into operation in the USA as National Airlines offers a 35% discount for tickets without food and drink service.

The hit musical *A Chorus Line* is first

Josephine Baker (shown here in 1949) dies on 12 April

April 1975

performed in New York City.

Tuesday 15: Portugal begins a programme of nationalisation and land reform.

Wednesday 16: Hosni Mubarak becomes Vice-President of Egypt.

Thursday 17: The Cambodian Civil War ends as communist rebels seize control of the capital, Pnomh Penh.

Friday 18: The 200th anniversary of Paul Revere's midnight ride, warning American revolutionaries of the approach of the British army, is celebrated in the USA.

A Khmer Rouge mugshot of a woman holding her baby. Both were later executed by communist forces in the Cambodian Genocide, which begins on 19 April.

The first acidophilus milk, modified for those with lactose intolerance, is launched.

Saturday 19: India launches its first satellite.

The Cambodian Genocide begins as the Khmer Rouge communist forces round up all former government employees into concentration camps.

Sunday 20: Peter Schaeffer's play *Equus* wins the Tony Award for Best Play.

Monday 21: The Prime Minister of Cambodia, Long Boret, is executed by Khmer Rouge communist rebels.

Tuesday 22: Oswaldo Lopez Arellano is removed from office as President of Honduras following bribery allegations.

Dr Who star William Hartnell dies on 23 April.

April 1975

A US Marine escorts a South Vietnamese helicopter pilot and his family to safety during the evacuation of Saigon. The city falls to the communists on 30 April.

The logo of the terrorist group Red Army Faction, which bombs a West Germany embassy on 24 April.

Wednesday 23: The US Senate approves the use of American troops to oversee humanitarian aid to South Vietnam.

Actor William Hartnell, famous for playing the first Doctor Who, dies aged 67.

Thursday 24: Communist terrorists of the Red Army Faction (also known as the Baader-Meinhoff Gang) take 11 hostages and kill two employees in the West German embassy in Stockholm, Sweden. The siege ends when the gang's bomb accidentally explodes, allowing the hostages to escape.

Friday 25: The Socialist Party under Mario Soares gains power in Portugal's first multiparty elections held since the 'Carnation Revolution' of 1974.

Saturday 26: Boxer George Foreman fights five opponents in succession in a televised bout in Toronto known as 'Foreman versus Five.'

Sunday 27: Duong van Minh is elected as President of South Vietnam.

April 1975

Mario Soares takes over Portugal on 25 April.

Monday 28: David Prosser, a lone security guard at the Israeli consulate in Johannesburg, kills three people and holds another 21 hostage in protest against Yitzhak Rabin's government. By speaking in different accents over the radio and firing from different windows he is able to convince police he is one of six terrorists. He is later captured alive and sentenced to 25 years in prison.

Tuesday 29: As communist forces surround Saigon, Operation Frequent Wind, the air evacuation of all American citizens from South Vietnam, begins.

Wednesday 30: The Fall of Saigon takes place, ensuring the victory of North Vietnamese (communist) forces in the Vietnam War. President Duong Van Minh surrenders to Viet Cong forces who take the city without opposition.

May 1975

David Beckham is born on 2 May.

Thursday 1: Hank Aaron of the Milwaukee Brewers sets a still-unsurpassed baseball record when he achieves 2,297 runs batted in.

Vauxhall launches the Chevette, Britain's first small hatchback car.

Friday 2: The last remaining South Vietnamese forces surrender to the Viet Cong at Long Xuyen.

The footballer David Beckham is born in Leytonstone, London.

Saturday 3: Chairman Mao Zedong, ruler of China, calls for a reversal of the country's 'cultural revolution' in which many people were killed and imprisoned for criticism of the communist regime.

West Ham United beats Fulham 2-0 in the FA Cup Final at Wembley Stadium, London.

Sunday 4: The one millionth home run in major league baseball is scored by Bob Watson of the Houston Astros.

Moe Howard, the last of the Three Stooges comedy group, dies aged 77.

May 1975

Monday 5: Television broadcasting begins in South Africa.

Tuesday 6: A tornado destroys much of the city of Omaha, Nebraska. It is estimated as the costliest tornado in history, causing $300m in damage, but only killing three people.

Cardinal Joszef Mindszenty, a symbol of resistance to the communist regime in Hungary, dies aged 77.

Wednesday 7: US President Ford declares the end of the US army's 'Vietnam Era', which began in 1961.

Sony launches the Betamax home video system on 10 May. A Betamax cassette is shown above (top) in contrast with the rival VHS system tapes launched in 1976.

Thursday 8: The last known remaining foreigners in Cambodia are expelled by the Khmer Rouge communist forces.

The singer Enrique Iglesias is born in Madrid, Spain.

Friday 9: Brian Oldfield (USA) sets the world shot put record at 75' (22.86m). Due to his professional status the record is officially unrecognised.

The Vauxhall Chevette is launched on 1 May.

May 1975

Above: US marines board the Mayaguez on 15 May.

Saturday 10: Sony launches the Betamax home video recording system.

Sunday 11: Bob Dylan, Joan Baez and Paul Simon headline a concert in New York's Central Park to mark the end of the Vietnam War.

Monday 12: The US merchant ship SS *Mayaguez* is seized in international waters off the coast of Cambodia by Khmer Rouge forces.

Tuesday 13: Richard Hollingshead, inventor of the drive in movie theatre, dies aged 75.

Wednesday 14: Transformer 1, the first full sized luxury electric car, is launched in the USA.

Thursday 15: 38 American servicemen are killed in an extensive operation to rescue the crew of the US merchant ship SS *Mayaguez*.

Mo Howard (centre), last surviving member of the Three Stooges, dies on 4 May.

May 1975

Filbert Bayi becomes the world's fastest man on 17 May.

Junko Tabei becomes the first woman to climb Mount Everest on 16 May.

Friday 16: The Kingdom of Sikkim, formerly one of the Princely States of the British Raj, becomes the 22nd state of India.

Scotland's 33 shire counties are reorganised into nine Regions as the Local Government (Scotland) Act 1973 goes into effect.

Junko Tabei of Japan becomes the first woman to reach the summit of Mount Everest.

Saturday 17: Filbert Bayi of Tanzania sets the world record for running a mile, at 3 minutes 51 seconds in Kingston, Jamaica.

Sunday 18: The Chinese writer Ding Ling is released from prison as the communist government continues its reversal of the Cultural Revolution.

Monday 19: A trial lasting six years begins between the US government and IBM over alleged violations of anti-trust laws. The case is eventually dropped.

British scientist Jane Goodall narrowly escapes capture by marxist guerillas during an attack on the Gombe Stream primate research laboratory in Tanzania.

Give A Little Love by the Bay City Rollers hits number one in the UK singles charts.

Tuesday 20: The US TV crime drama series *Adam-12* ends its run after 174 episodes.

May 1975

Martin Milner and Kent McCord star in *Adam 12*, which ends its long run on 20 May.

Barbara Hepworth dies on 21 May.

Wednesday 21: The British sculptor Barbara Hepworth dies aged 72 in a fire at her studio.

Thursday 22: The most lucrative contract in American football to this date ($4m for two seasons) is turned down by Joe Namath of the New York Jets.

Friday 23: Lebanon comes under military rule.

Saturday 24: The USSR launches the Soyuz 18 mission to the Salyut 4 space station.

Sunday 25: A total lunar eclipse is visible in parts of Australia, north and south America, and western Europe.

Bobby Unser wins the Indianapolis 500 motor race.

Monday 26: The rapper Lauryn Hill is born in Newark, New Jersey.

Glen Campbell releases his hit single *Rhinestone Cowboy*.

Tuesday 27: 33 people are killed in a coach crash at Dibbles Bridge, near Hebden, North Yorkshire. It is the deadliest British road accident to this date.

Wednesday 28: The Economic Community of West African States is created.

May 1975

Thursday 29: Gustav Husak becomes President of Czechoslovakia.

Friday 30: The Suez Canal re-opens, after having been blocked for eight years since the Six Day War of 1967.

Saturday 31: Communist rebels seize Savannakhet, the second city of Laos.

Right: Glen Campbell releases *Rhinestone Cowboy* on 26 May.

Left: the Bay City Rollers hit number one on 19 May with *Give A Little Love*.

June 1975

Sunday 1: US President Gerald Ford meets his Egyptian counterpart Anwar Sadat for talks in Salzburg, Austria. Ford falls over while descending the steps of Airforce One, leading to considerable negative publicity.

Monday 2: Snow falls on London, the first time it has snowed in the capital in summer since 1888.

Tuesday 3: Separate PE classes for boys and girls in US state schools are abolished.

The musical *Chicago* opens on Broadway, the first of 936 performances.

Whispering Grass by Don Estelle and Windsor Davies hits number one in the UK singles charts.

Wednesday 4: The actor and commentator Russell Brand is born in London.

Windsor Davies (left) and Don Estelle, stars of the BBC comedy series *It Ain't Half Hot Mum*, have an unlikely number one hit with *Whispering Grass* on 3 June.

June 1975

The actress Angelina Jolie is born in Los Angeles, California.

Thursday 5: In the first referendum held in the United Kingdom's history, voters choose to stay in the European Community (later the EU). Entry to the community took place in 1973 without a referendum.

Friday 6: A long term inmate of Southern Michigan Prison escapes by helicopter in a daring rescue attempt in broad daylight; he is recaptured two days later.

Saturday 7: Greece adopts a new constitution, formally replacing its monarchy with a republic.

Above: Pelé shows his ball control skills to US President Gerald Ford. The football star joins the New York Cosmos on 10 June.

The first Cricket World Cup for one day internationals begins in England; matches are held simultaneously in London, Birmingham, Leeds and Manchester.

Above: Angelina Jolie is born on 4 June.

Sunday 8: The USSR launches the Venera 9 space probe to Venus.

Monday 9: Proceedings in Britain's Houses of Parliament are broadcast on the radio for the first time.

Tuesday 10: The association footballer Edson Arantes do Nascimento (better known as Pelé) becomes the highest-paid athlete in the world when he joins the New York Cosmos for a fee of $4.7m for 107 matches.

June 1975

Wednesday 11: Britain's first North Sea oil rig goes into operation. North Sea oil and gas eventually lead to a regeneration of the country's depleted wealth.

Thursday 12: The first large-scale machine translation takes place, as the Systran computer in Zurich, Switzerland, translates 30,000 words of Russian into English.

Friday 13: Iran and Iraq sign a peace treaty in Algiers.

Saturday 14: The USSR launches the Venera 10 probe to Venus.

Above: Lord Lucan is pronounced guilty *in absentio* on 19 June.

Sunday 15: The black supremacist movement The Nation of Islam opens its membership to whites, announcing that they are now considered 'fully human.'

Brazilian footballer Pele makes his US debut, scoring a goal for the New York Cosmos in a 2-2 draw with Dallas Tornado.

Monday 16: Australia's Great Barrier Reef Marine Park is created.

Left: Transworld 58, Britain's first North Sea oil rig, under construction. It goes into operation on 11 June.

June 1975

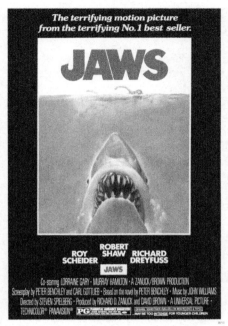

Above: the film *Jaws* is released on 20 June.

Tuesday 17: The Northern Mariana Islands in the Pacific Ocean become part of the USA.

A two-day long sandstorm causes major damage in Palm Springs, California.

Wednesday 18: Britain's Secretary of State for Energy, Anthony Wedgwood Benn officially turns on the supply of North Sea Oil.

Thursday 19: Mafia boss Sam Giancana is shot dead at his home Oak Park, Illinois, five days before he was due to testify before the US Congress on organised crime.

Constantine Tsatsos becomes the first elected President of Greece.

A coroner's court jury rules that Richard Bingham, Lord Lucan, murdered his family nanny, Sandra Rivett, in November 1974. Lucan, who disappeared after the killing, is declared officially dead in 1999.

Friday 20: The film *Jaws* is released in the USA; it soon becomes the highest-grossing film in history, until overtaken by Star Wars in 1977.

The former governor of California, Ronald Reagan, announces his intention to run for US President.

Saturday 21: McDonald's opens the first 'drive-through' restaurant in the USA, at Sierra Vista, Arizona.

June 1975

Idi Amin hits the headlines on 22 June.

The West Indies defeats Australia 291 to 274 to win the first ever Cricket World Cup at Lord's, London.

Sunday 22: Idi Amin, dictator of Uganda, calls off the execution of a British citizen, Denis Hills, after he wrote a newspaper article criticising the regime. Amin is persuaded by the arrival of his former commanding officers in the King's African Rifles, bearing a personal appeal for clemency by Queen Elizabeth II.

Monday 23: The rock singer Alice Cooper is badly injured in a fall from the stage at a concert in Vancouver, Canada.

Lou Graham wins the US Open golf championships at Medinah, Illinois.

Tuesday 24: 113 people are killed when Eastern Airlines Flight 66 crashes at New York JFK airport. The disaster is attributed to the newly discovered phenomenon of microbursts, sudden strong down-drafts of wind.

The claim of Don Juan de Borbon to the throne of Spain is turned down by the Spanish government, who instead announce that his son, Juan Carlos, will succeed General Franco as head of state.

As the Restoration of the Spanish monarchy gets underway, the claim of the heir apparent, Don Juan de Borbon (far left) is rejected by the government on 24 June in favour of his son, Juan Carlos (left).

June 1975

'Carlos the Jackal' escapes arrest on 27 June.

Wednesday 25: Portugal grants independence to its African colony of Mozambique.

Thursday 26: India's Prime Minister Indira Gandhi declares a state of emergency and rule by decree following calls for her resignation.

Friday 27: The international assassin, Ramirez Sanchez, better known as 'Carlos the Jackal' escapes arrest in Paris after shooting dead two policemen sent to detain him. He is eventually captured in 1994.

Golfers Lee Trevino and Jerry Heard are both hospitalised after being struck by lightning during the Western Open tournament in Oak Park, Illinois.

Saturday 28: The Anglo-Australian telescope, the largest in the southern hemisphere, goes into operation.

The screenwriter Rod Serling, best known for his series *The Twilight Zone*, dies aged 50.

Sunday 29: The environmentalist group Greenpeace makes its first sabotage attempt of a whaling ship.

Monday 30: Paul Biya becomes Prime Minister of Cameroon.

A 6.4 magnitude earthquake hits the Yellowstone National Park in Wyoming.

July 1975

Tuesday 1: ARPANET, the precursor to the internet, goes into operation.

37,000 New York City employees are made redundant in a round of budget cuts.

Wednesday 2: The actor James Robertson Justice, famous for the 'Doctor' series of comedy films, dies aged 68.

Thursday 3: The United States civil service bans discrimination against employees on grounds of sexual orientation.

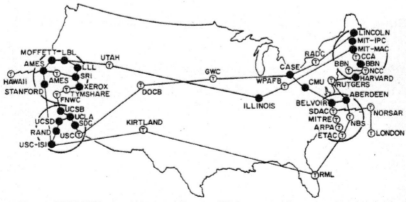

Above: ARPANET goes into operation on 1 July, connecting computers across the USA with links also to London.

July 1975

Friday 4: 13 people are killed in a bomb attack in Zion Square, Jerusalem, in the worst terror incident since Israel's founding in 1948.

Billie Jean King defeats Evonne Goolagong to win the Wimbledon ladies' tennis championships.

Saturday 5: The Cape Verde Islands are granted independence by Portugal.

Arthur Ashe beats Jimmy Connors to become the first black man to win Wimbledon.

The composer Dmitri Shostakovich completes his final composition, *Opus 147 Sonata for Viola and Piano*.

Sunday 6: The world stone-skimming record is set at 24 skips by Warren A. Klope on Lake Superior, Michigan.

The rapper '50 Cent' (Curtis Jackson) is born in New York City.

Monday 7: Alaska records its highest ever temperature, 90F (32C) at Juneau; it is one degree warmer than Miami Beach.

Tuesday 8: US President Gerald Ford announces he will run for office in 1976.

Above: Billie Jean King wins Wimbledon on 4 July with Arthur Ashe (top) gaining the men's title on 5 July.

A severe earthquake in Bagan, Burma, destroys most of the city's medieval temples.

Wednesday 9: Just four months before independence from Portugal, civil war breaks out in Angola between rival separatist groups.

July 1975

The last of the mighty Saturn rockets is launched on 15 July.

Yachtsman Bas Jan Ader of the Netherlands sets out to make the first solo west-east crossing of the North Atlantic. He is never seen again and his boat, *Ocean Wave*, is found off the Irish coast in April 1976.

Thursday 10: Britain's Foreign Secretary James Callaghan flies to Uganda to secure the release of British citizen Denis Hills, recently sentenced to death for criticising dictator Idi Amin.

Friday 11: Martin Cox of Sarasota, Florida, the longest-surviving liver-transplant patient, dies aged 17 six years after the operation.

Saturday 12: The west African island of Sao Tome and Principe is granted independence from Portugal.

Sunday 13: Two people are shot dead in sectarian violence in Belfast following a dispute between rival loyalist groups.

Above: Bruce Springsteen's album *Born to Run* is completed on 19 July.

July 1975

Monday 14: South Africa and the USA begin financial aid to western-aligned independence fighters in Angola.

Tuesday 15: The first Apollo mission since 1972 is launched, marking the last use of the enormous Saturn rocket on a manned mission.

Mujahadeen fighters in Afghanistan. Their uprising begins on 22 July.

Wednesday 16: The evacuation of Portuguese citizens from Angola begins.

Thursday 17: The first link-up in orbit of US and Soviet spacecraft takes place.

Friday 18: US President Gerald Ford secretly approves Operation IA Feature, a CIA plan to aid western-aligned guerilla in the Angolan Civil War.

Saturday 19: Bruce Springsteen and the E Street Band complete the album *Born to Run*.

Hatton Cross underground station opens in London, completing the first phase of the Piccadilly Line extension to Heathrow Airport.

Sunday 20: The syndicated newspaper cartoon strip Pogo is published for the last time after a 26-year run.

Monday 21: The Parliament of India votes to approve Prime Minister Indira Gandhi's declaration of a state of emergency.

July 1975

Liz Truss is born on 26 July.

Tuesday 22: An uprising by Mujahadeen rebels begins in Afghanistan.

Wednesday 23: Alan Ayckbourn's play *Absent Friends* opens in London.

Thursday 24: The Apollo space programme comes to an end, with the last 'splashdown' sea landing for more than 45 years. No further US manned space missions take place until 1981.

Friday 25: Portugal's Supreme Revolutionary Council, in charge since the country's 1974 revolution, hands over power to President General Francisco da Costa Gomes.

Above: Van McCoy hits number one in the USA with *The Hustle* on 26 July.

Saturday 26: The government of Ethiopia nationalises almost all its land, banning anyone from owning more than one house or 500 square metres of unoccupied land.

The Hustle by Van McCoy hits number one in the US charts.

Liz Truss, Britain's shortest-serving Prime Minister, is born in Oxford.

Sunday 27: Following the end of US involvement in the Vietnam War, the government of neighbouring Thailand ends all military agreements with the USA and gives notice to all US troops based in the country.

July 1975

Monday 28: The Turkish government, angered at a ban on military aid, orders the closure of all US military bases in the country.

Tuesday 29: Brigadier-General Murtala Mohammed seizes power in Nigeria in a military coup.

Wednesday 30: Trade union president Jimmy Hoffa goes missing near Detroit, Michigan. A convicted criminal with underworld connections, Hoffa is assumed to have been murdered by the Mafia; his body is never found.

The science fiction writer James Blish, known for his series of *Star Trek* adaptations, dies aged 54.

Thursday 31: Three members of the Irish pop group The Miami Showband are killed in a loyalist bomb attack in Newry, County Down.

August 1975

Friday 1: The Helsinki Accords, a 35-state treaty on human rights and national sovereignty in Europe are signed.

One of the oldest humanoid skulls, of the species *Homo ergaster*, is found in Kenya. It is approximately 1.75 million years old.

The British government introduces anti-inflation policies, as price increases reach 24.2%.

A reconstruction of a female *Homo ergaster*. One of the oldest skulls of this species is found on 1 August.

Saturday 2: Peace talks for Cyprus take place between Greek and Turkish factions in Vienna; it is agreed that population exchanges will take place under UN supervision.

Sunday 3: Italy's Vittorio Brambilla wins the Danish Grand Prix motor race.

Monday 4: 188 people are killed when a Royal Jordanian Airlines flight crashes near Agadir, Morocco.

Japanese Red Army terrorists seize 52 hostages in the American consulate in Kuala Lumpur, Malaysia.

August 1975

Agatha Christie's character of Hercule Poirot (shown here played by Peter Ustinov) is killed off by his creator in the novel *Curtain*, published on 6 August.

Tuesday 5: US President Gerald Ford posthumously restores the citizenship of General Robert E. Lee, who was stripped of it in 1865 following the defeat of his Confederate army.

Wednesday 6: The publication of Agatha Christie's new novel, *Curtain* is announced, in which her famous character Hercule Poirot is killed off.

Thursday 7: Typhoon Nina sets the record for typhoon rainfall when it deposits 38 inches (97 cm) of rain on Hebei Province in China.

The actress Charlize Theron is born in Benoni, South Africa.

Friday 8: 26,000 people are killed when the Banqiao Dam in Henan Province, China, bursts following heavy rainfall from Typhoon Nina. The disaster, the third largest flood in history, is kept secret by Chinese authorities until 2005.

The jazz saxophonist Cannonball Adderley dies aged 46.

Charlize Theron is born on 10 August.

Saturday 9: Mark Donohue sets the world speed record on a motor racing course at 221 mph in a Porsche 917.30 at Talledega Speedway, Alabama.

August 1975

The composer Dmitri Shostakovich dies aged 69.

Sunday 10: The 39th Amendment to the Constitution of India takes effect, allowing Prime Minister Indira Gandhi to rule by decree.

Monday 11: The British Leyland Motor Corporation comes under majority state ownership.

Civil war breaks out in the Portuguese colony of East Timor.

Above: British Leyland is nationalised on 11 August

Tuesday 12: John Walker of New Zealand sets the world record for running a mile at 3 minutes 49 seconds in Gothenburg, Sweden.

Wednesday 13: Five people are killed in an IRA bomb attack on the Bayardo Bar in Belfast.

An attempted military coup takes place in Libya against the rule of General Muammar Gaddafi

Thursday 14: Norway's Svalbard airport opens, the world's most northerly airport with scheduled flights.

Left: the Viking probe is prepared for its launch to Mars, which takes place on 20 August.

August 1975

Friday 15: President Sheikh Mujibur Rahman of Bangladesh is assassinated in a military coup.

The 'Birmingham Six' are sentenced to life imprisonment for IRA bomb attacks on two pubs in Birmingham in 1974. Their convictions are overturned in 1991.

Above: Haile Selassie, Emperor of Ethiopia, dies seemingly of natural causes on 27 November. It is not until 1994 that his death is discovered to have been an assassination.

Saturday 16: The serial killer Ted Bundy is arrested in Salt Lake County, Utah.

Can't Give You Anything (But My Love) by the Stylistics hits number one in the UK singles charts.

Sunday 17: Two fatal motor racing accidents take place on the same day; Tiny Lund is killed in the Talledega 500 in Alabama and Mark Donohue is fatally injured in the Austrian Grand Prix.

Monday 18: The largest forest fire in German history is put out after burning for ten days at Luneberg Heath. Five firemen are killed in the blaze and 18,300 acres (7418 hectares) of forest are destroyed.

Tuesday 19: Headingley Cricket Ground in Leeds is vandalised by campaigners for the release of armed robber George Davis.

Wednesday 20: NASA launches the Viking 1 probe to Mars. It reaches the surface of the Red Planet in July 1976.

Thursday 21: The US government partially lifts its trade embargo against communist Cuba.

August 1975

Composer Dmitri Shostakovich dies on 9 August.

Friday 22: The Argentinian navy ship *Santisima Trinidad* is sunk in La Plata Harbour by terrorists of the far left Montoneros group.

Saturday 23: Laos becomes the third nation in Indochina to fall under communist rule, as Pathet Lao guerillas seize control of the capital, Ventiane.

Sunday 24: Colonels Pattakos, Makarezos and Papadopolous, who staged the 'Colonels' Coup' in Greece in 1967, are sentenced to death (later commuted to life imprisonment).

Charles Revson, founder of the Revlon cosmetics company, dies aged 68.

Monday 25: Bruce Springsteen's album *Born to Run* is released.

Ian Smith, leader of Rhodesia's white minority government, meets for talks with Bishop Abel Muzorewa, leader of the black majority African National Council, in the hope of avoiding civil war.

Tuesday 26: Bahrain returns to rule by decree after a two-year experiment in representative democracy.

Wednesday 27: Haile Selassie, the exiled last Emperor of Ethiopia is reported to have died of natural causes. In 1994 a court rules that he was in fact murdered by members of the opposition Derg regime.

Thursday 28: In the face of rising nationalist violence, Mario Lemos Pires, governor of Portuguese East Timor, abandons the colony with 722 refugees.

Friday 29: General Francisco Morales Bermudez seizes control of Peru in a military coup.

August 1975

Above: General Bermudez seizes control of Peru on 29 August.

The second brightest nova (new star) of the 20th century, V1500 Cygni, becomes visible to the naked eye on earth.

Eamon de Valera, former President of Ireland, dies aged 92.

Saturday 30: The Convention on the Prevention of Marine Pollution goes into force.

Sunday 31: The largest bus robbery in history takes place as 38 people are deprived of $35,000 in cash and valuables when thieves hold up a Greyhound coach in Detroit, Michigan.

September 1975

Above: 1976 *Space 1999* TV-tie-in annual. The popular series, produced by *Thunderbirds* creators Gerry and Sylvia Anderson, is first shown on 1 September.

Monday 1: 30 people are killed in an attempted military coup in Ecuador.

The TV science-fiction series *Space: 1999* is first broadcast.

Concorde becomes the first aeroplane to cross the Atlantic four times in a single day.

Tuesday 2: The Ho Chi Minh Mausoleum opens in Hanoi, Vietnam.

Wednesday 3: The Fourth Test between England and Australia at the Oval cricket ground, London, ends in a draw.

September 1975

Thursday 4: The Sinai Interim Agreement between Israel and Egypt is signed in Geneva, leading to the establishment of a 15-mile buffer zone between the two countries in the Sinai Desert.

Friday 5: Lynette Fromme, a member of the Charles Manson 'Family' cult, attempts to shoot US President Gerald Ford in Sacramento, California. Fromme's attempt fails when she forgets to cock her pistol. She is later sentenced to 34 years in prison.

Two people are killed in an IRA bomb attack on the London Hilton Hotel.

Saturday 6: Over 2000 people are killed when a 6.7 magnitude earthquake hits Diyarbakir, Turkey.

Rod Stewart tops the charts on 6 September.

Sailing by Rod Stewart hits number one in the UK singles charts.

Niki Lauda wins the World Driving Championship on 7 September.

Sunday 7: Formula 1 star Niki Lauda (Austria) wins the World Driving Championship.

Monday 8: Cuban merchant vessels are admitted to US ports for refueling for the first time since 1961.

Tuesday 9: The comedy series *Welcome Back, Kotter* is first broadcast on US TV. The show launches the career of John Travolta.

The first national beer exhibition is held in London by CAMRA, the Campaign for Real Ale, in response to the poor quality of beer in many British pubs.

September 1975

The singer Michael Buble is born in Burnaby, British Columbia.

Wednesday 10: Viking 2, the second NASA Mars probe is launched.

Thursday 11: The serial killer Joseph James DeAngelo, aka 'The Night Stalker', claims his first victim in Exeter, California.

Friday 12: The album *Wish You Were Here* is released by Pink Floyd.

Saturday 13: Argentina's president, Eva Peron, begins a month's leave of absence due to mental health problems.

Sunday 14: Elizabeth Ann Seton (1774-1821) is canonised by the Roman Catholic Church, making her the first American saint.

Rembrandt's painting *The Night Watch* is slashed by a mentally disturbed man in the Rijksmuseum, Amsterdam.

Monday 15: Chris Balderstone becomes the first and only man to play in a first class cricket match (Leicestershire v Derbyshire) and a football match (Doncaster Rovers v Brentford) on the same day.

Tuesday 16: Martin Cooper of Motorola is granted the first patent for a hand-held mobile telephone.

Papua New Guinea is granted independence from Australia.

The Soviet Mikoyan MiG-31 'Foxhound' jet fighter is first flown.

Above: inventor Martin Cooper demonstrates his prototype mobile phone, for which he receives a patent on 16 September.

Wednesday 17: A taser is used for the first time in a robbery, when thieves use it to incapacitate a petrol station attendant in Miami Shores, Florida.

September 1975

The Mikoyan MiG-31 is first flown on 16 September.

A bank in Traverse City, Michigan, mistakenly exchanges a 1923 German 100,000 Reichmark note (worth less than one US cent) at the present-day rate for the Deutschmark ($39,700). The customer, Stephen Holcomb, is later sued by the bank but is only able to return $18,177, having spent the rest.

Thursday 18: The bank robber Patricia Hearst, grand-daughter of newspaper magnate William Randolph Hearst, is arrested in San Francisco. Originally kidnapped by a far-left terror group in 1974, she later sided with them to commit a series of robberies. She is pardoned in 2001.

Friday 19: The communist leadership of Cambodia abolishes the use of money and closes all schools.

The first episode of the comedy series *Fawlty Towers* is broadcast on the BBC.

Saturday 20: *Fame* by David Bowie hits the top of the charts in the USA, making it the singer's first American number one hit.

Right: the kidnap victim turned bank-robber Patricia Hearst is arrested on 18 September.

September 1975

Sunday 21: Sultan Yahya Petra of Kelantan becomes the elected sovereign of Malaysia.

Monday 22: A second assassination attempt is made on US President Gerald Ford by Sara Jane Moore in San Francisco. After firing one shot at the President which misses, Moore is overpowered by a member of the public.

Tuesday 23: As part of a clampdown on religion, the government of Albania requires anyone with a Christian, Muslim or Hebrew name to change it to an approved secular alternative.

Wednesday 24: Dougal Haston and Doug Scott become the first Britons to climb Everest.

Thursday 25: The TV presenter Declan Donnelly (Dec of Ant and Dec) is born in Newcastle upon Tyne.

German diver Joachim Welder, 36, a crew member of the Helgoland Underwater Habitat research station in the Gulf of Maine, dies of an embolism after ascending from a dive.

The Pink Floyd album *Wish You Were Here* reaches number one in the US charts.

Friday 26: The film The Rocky Horror Picture Show is first shown in cinemas. It gains a cult following in 1976 when a trend begins to watch it with audience participation, and becomes the longest running theatrical release film in cinema history.

Saturday 27: The last executions take place in Spain as five Basque separatists are shot by firing squad. Spain abolishes the death penalty in 1978.

President Ford recoils in shock as a shot is fired at him on 22 September.

September 1975

The AH-64 Apache makes its first flight on 30 October.

Sunday 28: The Spanish missionary John Macias (1585-1645) is canonised by the Roman Catholic Church.

The first Long Beach Grand Prix is held in Long Beach, California.

Monday 29: The singer Jackie Wilson collapses and falls into a coma after a performance in Cherry Hill, New Jersey. He never regains consciousness and dies in 1984.

Tuesday 30: The AH-64 Apache helicopter makes its first flight.

October 1975

Wednesday 1: The 'Thriller in Manila' takes place as Muhammed Ali retains his boxing World Heavyweight title against Joe Frazer in Manila, Phillippines.

Thursday 2: The W.T. Grant department store chain, one of America's largest with 1000 stores, goes into administration.

The Chevrolet Chevette, one of the first economical sub-compact cars, is launched in the USA.

The loyalist paramilitary group The Ulster Volunteer Force kills seven people in a series of attacks across Northern Ireland.

Friday 3: Guy Mollet, former Prime Minister of France, dies aged 69.

George Harrison's album *Extra Texture* is released

Saturday 4: The Paris Motor Show opens. Models launched include the Simca 1307, sold in Britain as the Talbot Alpine.

Hold Me Close by David Essex hits number one in the UK singles chart.

The Chevrolet Chevette is launched in the USA on 2 October.

October 1975

The Simca 1307, badged in Britain as the Talbot Alpine, is launched on 4 October.

Sunday 5: The Algerian nuthatch bird (*sitta ledanti*) is discovered.

The actress Kate Winslet (*Titanic*) is born in Reading Berkshire.

An 11 year old girl, Lesley Molseed, is murdered in West Yorkshire. Her killer is wrongly identified as Stefan Kiszko, who serves 16 years in prison before his conviction is overturned. In 2006 a DNA match leads to the conviction of Ronald Castree for the killing.

Below: Kate Winslet is born on 5 October.

Monday 6: The US Secret Service announces two men involved in a plot to assassinate Japan's Emperor Hirohito during a state visit have been arrested in New York City.

Tuesday 7: 27 people are killed in far-left terror attacks in Argentina, by members of the outlawed Montoneros group.

The singer John Lennon wins a legal battle to avoid deportation from the USA.

Wednesday 8: The South Korean serial killer, Kim Dae-doo, is arrested after claiming 17 victims.

Women are admitted for the first time to the US Service Academies for officer training.

Thursday 9: Andrei Sakharov of the USSR is awarded the Nobel Peace Prize.

October 1975

The singer Sean Lennon, son of John Lennon and Yoko Ono, is born in New York City.

Friday 10: Domestic airmail ends as a separate postal service in the USA, with all long distance domestic post sent by air.

Elizabeth Taylor and Richard Burton remarry in a ceremony in Botswana, two years after their divorce. They divorce again in 1976.

Elizabeth Taylor and Richard Burton: the celebrity couple remarry on 10 October.

Saturday 11: The satirical series *Saturday Night Live* is first broadcast in the USA, hosted by George Carlin.

The future US President Bill Clinton marries Hilary Rodham in Fayetteville, Arkansas.

Sunday 12: Oliver Plunkett (1629-1681) becomes the first Irishman to be canonised by the Roman Catholic Church since 1225 AD.

A large bomb is defused by police at Lockett's restaurant in London; it is thought the target may have been the flat above, occupied by MI6 director Maurice Oldfield.

The Vauxhall Cavalier is launched at the Earl's Court Motor Show on 14 October

October 1975

Monday 13: The first dollar coin with no silver content is issued in the USA, to commemorate the country's bicentennial.

Tuesday 14: Six people are killed when an RAF Avro Vulcan bomber crashes at Zabbar, Malta.

The Earl's Court Motor Show in London opens; models launched include the Vauxhall Cavalier.

Wednesday 15: The Metropolitan Police use a special robot to examine the bomb planted at Lockett's restaurant on 12 October.

Thursday 16: Five Australian TV journalists are killed by Indonesian forces invading East Timor.

The first grainy pictures of the surface of Venus are sent back to Earth by the Venera probe on 22 October.

Friday 17: The band Roxy Music performs at the Empire Pool, London, as part of their world tour.

Saturday 18: The singer Lionel Richie marries Brenda Harvey.

Sunday 19: The last games of the short-lived American World Football League take place. Intended to bring the game to a global audience, the only team outside the continental US was from Hawaii.

Monday 20: 43 people are killed in an underground railway crash in Mexico City, Mexico.

October 1975

Tuesday 21: The 1,160m Tanzam Railroad spanning Tanzania and Zambia opens.

Spain's dictator, Francisco Franco, suffers a major heart attack.

Wednesday 22: The first photographs of the surface of another planet are beamed back to Earth as the Venera 9 probe lands on Venus.

The historian Arnold Toynbee dies aged 86.

Thursday 23: The cancer specialist Gordon Fairley is killed by accident when he walks past an IRA car bomb intended for Hugh Fraser MP in London. Fraser escapes unharmed.

Peter Sutcliffe, AKA the Yorkshire Ripper, claims his first victim on 30 October.

Friday 24: The Turkish Ambassador to France, Ismail Erez, is assassinated by Armenian militants in Paris.

Saturday 25: Venera 10 becomes the second space probe to land on Venus.

38 people are arrested and 102 injured as serious disorder breaks out at a football match in West Ham, London.

Sunday 26: Justin de Jacobis (1800-1860) is canonised by the Roman Catholic Church.

Monday 27: Five people are killed in a school shooting in Ottawa, Canada.

The crime author Rex Stout, creator of the fictional detective Nero Wolfe, dies aged 88.

Freddy Mercury of Queen. Their single *Bohemian Rhapsody* is released on 31 October.

October 1975

Tuesday 28: The French boxer Charles Carpentier dies aged 82. *Dr No* becomes the first James Bond film to be broadcast on British television.

Wednesday 29: US President Gerald Ford vetoes a federal bailout for the financially ailing New York City council.

Thursday 30: Peter Sutcliffe, the serial killer known as the Yorkshire Ripper, claims his first victim in Leeds.

King Juan Carlos I becomes head of state in Spain, after the dictator General Franco becomes too ill to govern.

Friday 31: Queen releases their hit single *Bohemian Rhapsody.*

November 1975

Saturday 1: US President Gerald Ford submits a video-taped testimony in the trial of Lynette Fromme, who attempted to assassinate him on 5 September.

Sunday 2: An estimated £100,000 of damage is caused in an arson attack on the Royal Pavilion, Brighton.

Monday 3: General Khaled Mosharraf seizes power in a military coup in Bangladesh.

Good Morning America is first broadcast on ABC-TV, hosted by David Harman and Nancy Dussault.

Tuesday 4: Cuban leader Fidel Castro sends 350 troops to Angola to support marxist rebels.

Wednesday 5: Punk rock is introduced to Britain as the Sex Pistols give their first public performance at St Martin's School of Art in London.

Below: Lynda Carter first appears as Wonder Woman on 7 November.

November 1975

Johnny Rotten of the Sex Pistols: the group makes its debut on 5 November.

Thursday 6: 524,000 unarmed Moroccan civilians occupy neighbour Spanish Sahara in an orchestrated land grab. Spain relinquishes its claim on the territory eight days later.

Friday 7: The TV series *Wonder Woman* starring Lynda Carter is first aired in the USA.

Saturday 8: A mutiny takes place on the Soviet frigate *Storozhevoy*. The mutiny, which fails, is the inspiration for the 1984 Tom Clancy novel, *The Hunt for Red October*.

Sunday 9: King Hassan II of Morocco calls off the civil invasion of neighbouring Spanish Sahara, ordering those occupying the territory to return home.

Monday 10: The Treaty of Osimo is signed, resolving ownership of the disputed city of Trieste; part of the territory goes to Italy, with the majority coming under Yugoslavian control.

Tuesday 11: Portugal grants independence to Angola, after five hundred years of colonial rule.

A constitutional crisis begins in Australia when the Governor-General, Sir John Kerr dismisses the Prime Minister, Gough Whitlam using the Royal Prerogative.

November 1975

Crown under: Australia is plunged into constitutional crisis on 11 November when Governor General Sir John Kerr (left), acting as proxy to HM Queen Elizabeth II, dismisses Prime Minister Gough Whitlam (right).

Wednesday 12: The longest serving United States Supreme Court Justice, William O. Douglas, retires after 36 years' service.

The conciliation service ACAS is set up in Britain to arbitrate in economic disputes.

Thursday 13: The 'Cod War' fishing rights dispute starts up again between Britain and Iceland.

The playwright R.C. Sherriff (*Journey's End*) dies aged 79.

Friday 14: Spain abandons its territory of the Spanish Sahara, to be divided between neighbouring Morocco and Mauritania.

Saturday 15: The G6 (Group of Six) economic forum holds its first summit in France, comprising France, Britain, West Germany Japan, Italy and the USA.

Sunday 16: The G6 summit announces a 'remarkable convergence of views' and predicts the worst of the economic slump is over.

Monday 17: The USSR launches the Soyuz 20 unmanned

November 1975

spacecraft for an endurance test; it remains in orbit for 90 days.

Tuesday 18: A total lunar eclipse is visible across the USA, Europe, Africa, Asia and western Australia.

Wednesday 19: The film *One Flew Over The Cuckoo's Nest* starring Jack Nicholson is released in the USA.

Thursday 20: Spain's dictator General Francisco Franco dies after 36 years in power.

The US government admits that the CIA twice tried to assassinate the Cuban leader Fidel Castro.

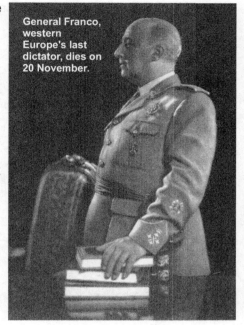

General Franco, western Europe's last dictator, dies on 20 November.

Friday 21: Labour MPs go on strike at the House of Commons over proposals by their party to send a senior Cabinet minister to the funeral of Spain's General Franco.

Saturday 22: King Juan Carlos I of Spain accedes to the throne.

Billy Connolly's comedy single *D.I.V.O.R.C.E.* hits number one in the UK singles charts.

7 people are killed when the USS *Belknap* collides with the USS *John F. Kennedy* off the coast of Sicily.

Sunday 23: The funeral of General Francisco Franco is held in Madrid.

Monday 24: Antonio Echeverria, the mayor of Oyarzun, Spain, is assassinated by Basque separatists.

November 1975

Tuesday 25: Dutch Guiana is granted independence from the Netherlands.

A failed military coup takes place in Portugal.

Wednesday 26: US President Gerald Ford approves a package of $2.3 bn in loans for New York City.

Thursday 27: Ross McWhirter, co-founder of the *Guinness Book of Records* and twin brother of TV presenter Norris McWhirter, is killed by IRA gunmen at his home in London.

Robert Muldoon becomes New Zealand PM on 29 November.

Friday 28: Portuguese Timor declares independence from Portugal as the Democratic Republic of East Timor.

Saturday 29: Robert Muldoon becomes Prime Minister of New Zealand.

The racing driver Graham Hill, 46, dies when his light aircraft crashes near Elstree, Hertfordshire.

Bohemian Rhapsody by Queen hits number one in the UK singles charts.

Sunday 30: The African nation of Dahomey changes its name to Benin.

Left: racing driver Graham Hill is killed in an air crash on 29 November.

December 1975

Monday 1: King Sissavang Vatthana of Laos abdicates following the communist takeover of his country; he and the rest of the royal family are initially allowed their freedom but later deported to a prison camp.

Tuesday 2: Two people are killed when Indonesian rebels take a passenger train hostage at Beilen in the Netherlands.

Wednesday 3: Gunmen seize control of a Credit Lyonnaise Bank in Paris. They are given a $2.2m ransom but are arrested after crashing their getaway car.

HM King Sissavang of Laos abdicates on 1 December.

Thursday 4: Indonesian rebels begin a 15 day hostage siege in the Indonesian consulate in Amsterdam, Netherlands.

Friday 5: Internment of suspected terrorists without trial is ended in Northern Ireland.

December 1975

Saturday 6: The six-day Balcombe Street Siege begins in London, as four IRA terrorists take two people hostage in a flat in London.

Sunday 7: Indonesian forces invade the newly independent territory of East Timor.

The US novelist and playwright Thorton Wilder (*Our Town*) dies aged 78.

Monday 8: 37 people are killed as the Lebanese Civil War intensifies in Beirut.

Tuesday 9: The United Nations issues the Declaration on the Rights of Disabled Persons.

Malcolm Fraser becomes Prime Minister of Australia on 13 December.

Wednesday 10: The Western Saharan separatist group, the Polisario, begins attacks on occupying Mauritanian troops.

Thursday 11: The US government issues a proposal to withdraw 1000 nuclear warheads from western Europe if the Soviets commit to removing 1700 tanks.

Friday 12: Satcom-1, the USA's third domestic communications satellite, is put into orbit.

The World Trade Center's observation deck opens on 14 December.

Saturday 13: Elections are held in Australia following the dissolution of Parliament by the Governor-General on behalf of the Queen. Malcolm Fraser's Liberal Party is elected.

December 1975

Left: 112 Ocean Drive, Amityville, NY. The alleged haunting known as the 'Amityville Horror' is said to have begun here on 18 December.

Sunday 14: The observation deck of the World Trade Center in New York City opens.

Pope John Paul VI offers a symbolic reconciliation between the Roman Catholic Church and Eastern Orthodox Church. The two denominations separated in the Great Schism of 1054 AD.

Monday 15: New Zealand's Prime Minister Robert Muldoon announces an end to the country's state pension scheme.

Tuesday 16: Sara Jane Moore pleads guilty to the attempted assassination of US President Gerald Ford on 22 September. She goes on to serve 32 years in prison.

Wednesday 17: The UNESCO World Heritage Convention for the protection of historic buildings and sites is ratified.

Thursday 18: George and Kathleen Lutz and their children move into a supposedly haunted house at 112 Ocean Drive, Amityville, New York. Their experiences lead to the bestselling book and film *The Amityville Horror.*

Friday 19: Argentina's President Isabel Peron is forced to resign by a military junta.

Saturday 20: Britain announces cuts of 3500 men from its Hong Kong garrison following a new defence agreement for the colony.

December 1975

Sunday 21: Eleven energy ministers are taken hostage by Palestinian terrorists at the Vienna headquarters of OPEC (Organisation of Petroleum Exporting Countries). The hostages are released after a reported ransom of US$50m.

Monday 22: The US governments sets up the Strategic Petroleum Reserve, an emergency stockpile of 714 million barrels of oil.

Tuesday 23: 21 people are killed by a single bolt of lightning in Rhodesia (now Zimbabwe). It remains the deadliest lightning strike on record.

The US Metric Conversion Act goes into effect, intending a gradual voluntary switch from the Imperial to Metric systems of measurement, but the idea does not catch on.

Wednesday 24: The British government announces a sharp rise in unemployment, with the jobless total in excess of 1.2 million.

Thursday 25: *The Wizard of Oz* is broadcast on British television for the first time.

The heavy metal band Iron Maiden is formed in London.

Friday 26: The Soviet supersonic jet liner the Tupolev Tu-144, nicknamed the 'Russian Concorde', goes into service.

Saturday 27: India's worst mining disaster takes place as 372 miners die in a cave-in at Dhanband, Jharkand.

Sunday 28: The Icelandic coastguard vessel *Tyr* rams the Royal Navy's HMS *Andromeda* in the

Right: Isabel Peron is forced to resign on 19 December.

December 1975

first confrontation of the Third Cod War over fishing rights in the north Atlantic.

Monday 29: Eleven people are killed in a bomb attack at La Guardia airport, New York City. No group claims responsibility.

Tuesday 30: The golfer Tiger Woods is born in Cypress, California.

Oleg Blokhin of Dynamo Kiev is awarded the Ballon d'Or for Best European Footballer.

Wednesday 31: France grants independence to its African island colony of Comoros.

The Tupolev Tu-144 goes into service on 26 December.

Printed in Great Britain
by Amazon